hummin~~

sophia ela__e hanson

HUMMINGBIRD
ISBN-13: 978-0578189277
Cover Design: Docshot
Printing: Createspace
Print and eBook Formatting: Heather Adkins
Illustrations: Munise Sertel (instagram.com/mns_art)
Copyright: 2017 Calida Lux Publishing

*For the person I am
learning to be*

Part I

Memory is a strange beast. It looks different to everyone who lays eyes on it. Its teeth are as sharp as its coat is downy. I wonder what you remember, what you see when you say my name in the cold place between day and night. Do you still say it? Can you? Do I reply?

- *Animals*

Hello and a flash of
Big teeth. Eye contact
That lasts a bit too long
To be anything but
something.

- *I was thinking about the
first time I saw you*

You are very good at
talking
Without saying a word.

- *Your mouth*

You call me hummingbird,
A heart too big for my
little ribs.

- *Hummingbird heart*

You ask me what my favorite song is. I tell you *Penelope*, because it feels like it is coming out of me rather than going in. A day later, you call and play the entire thing on your rickety piano. This is when I know you love me.

- *Penelope*

You are the only one I can
sleep with.
You are my slow breath, my
white noise, my dappled
sky.

- *4:05 A.M.*

Your mattress sags in the middle. We cannot sleep apart. When we try, we roll back into the ravine like Jack and Jill. Not that we mind. We never seem to be close enough.

- *To fetch a pail of water*

You smell like winter and dust,
But not the kind that comes from the stars.

- *You are winter*

You rarely say it.
For you it is
Stepping out on the ice
In the middle of March.
You brush away my tears
Like dried wax.
When your lips split I
hear a
Deafening crack.
The cold water hits and I
am warm.

- *Three words*

We are quite good at the whole distance thing. Every Friday we exchange gifts over FaceTime. I write you poems. You write me songs. I paint, you sketch. Sometimes. Other times, we just take our clothes off and pretend we are ten states closer.

- *Exchange rate*

I wanted to tell you
That you laugh like June
And sing like winter.
Pure, cool, and ragged.

- *I wanted to tell you*

You remind me
I am full of all the
Ecstatic beauty
I see in you.

- *Full*

In the morning when my
hair
Is half plastered to my
scalp,
Half spastic with static.
When my eyeliner crusts
like
Icelandic sand beneath my
lashes.
When I am over you or
under.
When you can feel my words
on
Your skin or when they
cloud on
The lens of my iPhone.

- *You call me lovely*

Everything is stale.
Our breath,
The whole grain bread we
popped in the toaster.
You hoist me onto the
countertop,
Kiss me through the film
of sleep
While we wait for the
Twang of springs.

- *Breakfast, 10:07 A.M.*

You find out by accident. I
would have told you
eventually. Instead, you
touch me in just the right
way and send me reeling
back into the past. You
could not have known. You
cradle me to your chest,
soaking up the tremors and
confessions and fears until
I am clean.

- *Clean*

You do not complete me,
You wrap around me.

- *What I tell you when
your fears creep in*

Every week you have a different dream. You say it works for you. Maybe it does. I tell my friends you are the type of person who will figure himself out at 32.

- *I still believe that*

Can we pretend
We are robbers?
I will bring
The water pistols,
You bring the masks.

- *Balaclavas*

When I was fifteen I got sick. No cure, only treatment. When I was sixteen I was assaulted. I used to joke that at least I got the bad stuff out of the way early, as if there was a cap on how much pain a person could endure over the course of their life.

- *Obviously, I had never been in love*

Ozone in the air before a
lightning strike.
Brown spots on a banana
before it turns to mush.
A tickle in my throat
before a cold sets in.

- *You gave me no such
warning*

Interlude

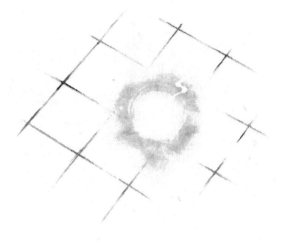

There once was a girl who carried her soul in the palm of her hand. When she was born, her tiny pink fingers unfurled and a little ball of white light tumbled out. It rolled across the hospital bed and landed on the tiles, tinkling like a bell. A crack formed in its curved walls. From then on, she had to be extra careful, lest something terrible crawl in or leak out.

Like any other child she grew up slowly, then all at once. She took to carrying her soul in a pouch around her neck. It beat against her sternum when she ran, its radiance bleeding through the fabric.

Her soul made her honest. Her soul made her kind. It made her swerve for pedestrian ants when she rode her bicycle through the suburbs. It made her cry when she found a sparrow dead on the sidewalk. She moved it into the grass with a stick and covered it in petals. You see, our skin should do more than just protect our bones.

She grew weary of the weight around her neck. Her head was bowed when he came along and lifted the soul in its pouch. The string went slack. He held it up to the sun, squinting at the joint radiance. What a beautiful burden, he said.

– *The radiance*

Part II

You tell me about her in fragments, like you are spitting out chunks of glass. A passing comment here, a quiet moment there. We all know silence is louder than noise. She haunts you like bad breath. Every time I make you laugh, I think she recedes. Every time we kiss, I think I exorcise her. You think so too, for awhile.

- *Silence and noise*

I have this feeling
That you like me crying
Even if you do not know
it.

- *Pretty when I cry*

My love is not some
garment
To hang on the coatrack
Until you are cold enough
To wear it.

- *Threadbare*

You are so careful with my
body.
What about my brain?

- *Missing the point*

I start to feel
I should be grateful
Just to breathe in
The words you
So generously exhale.

- *I start to act like it,
too*

Your eyes, oncoming
headlights.
Your fingers, pill bugs.
Your words, wires around
my ankles.

- *1:14 A.M.*

That night I lose time, whole hours you swallow up with your words. You say this is not one of my books, there is no pretty ribbon to tie up the end. You are so calm. I wish you would rage. Then, I could storm out on the heels of righteous betrayal. I could pretend I do not know she still clings to you like a parasite. I wish you would rage. Instead, you let me rot back to life on your floor. I call my dad. He drives me home and picks up my car the next morning.

- *Rot*

My sheets still smell like
winter and dust.

- *2:03 A.M.*

Each second a scab
I cannot stop picking.
I get in the shower
And climb into the
hurricane
Prowling the drain.

- *The morning after*

Time stretches and warps.
I want to split it with a
knife.
I want to flay it with my
fingernails.

- *The weeks after*

I do not notice
Until I stand on the scale
Half a month later.

- *You are eating me alive*

You took so much so fast.
You did not bother to
stitch my wounds.
I spread my insides on the
floor,
Step back and admire
The awful mess you made of
me.

- *Spread*

When you would kiss me on
the brow,
The stars and the planets
long since hidden,
They would bow.

- Bow

I sit in the silence of
subway cars
And the spaces between
songs.
I walk in the wake of dusk
Where the grass is cool
and damp.

- *Cold places*

I kiss a stranger.
I thought I was looking
for you.

- *I was looking for myself*

Hate is easy.

- You are harder

I am playing my part, just
like you.

- *When he asks me why I am
so kind*

For every star I scrape
From the canvas
A bit of indigo collects
Beneath my nails.

- *Extremis*

I wish I could live
On a plain.
Instead, I lose you
Somewhere in the
Ravines carved
In my mind.

- *Valleys and Peaks*

I love you. Come back.

*- He sends me a message
six months later*

I love you. No.

- *I respond*

If I could peel back
My skin, wrest open
My ribs, brush aside
My arteries like vines,
You would see
The misshapen organ you
Left behind.
It is a different animal.
It craves not your touch,
But the ink
That drains from the sky.

- *Animals II*

If loneliness was weakness
We would have
Withered long ago.

- *The human condition*

I am reclaiming
The restaurants,
The bars, the parks, the
storefronts crosshatched
With your fingerprints.
I fold the memories into
Cranes, tuck them away.

– *Making room*

The thing about the heart
Is that when it grows
back,
It takes a different
shape.
You molded mine into a
form
Perfect for someone new.

- *Lifeforms*

They have a face like
A light leak,
A body like a prayer,
And a soul like thunder.

- *My next lover*

I am learning
How to be my own sky.

- *Resurrection fern*

I never planned to release any of these poems. They were simply my way of dealing with what I had lost and reminding myself of what I still had. I realized though that if I kept them under lock and key they would fester. They needed to breathe. When my words breathe, I breathe. I am still breathing. You are, too.

Acknowledgements

This book was a whirlwind project that came into being one night in December, 2016. There are so many people to thank, but I need to keep this short.

First and foremost, I want to thank my mother. My biggest supporter, my first editor, and my cover designer. You inspire me to be more. I love you.

Next, I want to thank my dad, who is there for me through everything. I have no idea what I would do without you. I love you.

Munise, the incredible artist who drew the illustrations throughout this book. Thank you so much for your creativity and enthusiasm.

My friends. Allie, Dani, Emma, Annmarie, Mackenzie, Grace, Kosta, Maya, Jill, Eniola, Brandon, Jennifer, Dela. You lift me. I love you.

My family, who accepts me as I am. I love you.

My readers, my Anthemites. Thank you for breathing life into my books. I am the luckiest author in the world.

And to my first love, I hope you find another bird.

62677154R00046

Made in the USA
Lexington, KY
14 April 2017